Person-Centered Counseling

An Example Case Study for the Beginning Therapist

B. L. LARSEN

ISBN-10: 1507553307
ISBN-13: 978-1507553305

Contents

Contents

PURPOSE OF THIS BOOK

Learning how to apply a particular counseling theory is a difficult undertaking. Reading about the origins, history, and general framework of a theory is the obvious place to start, but how do you take all that knowledge and put it into practice in a real-life therapy room? The purpose of this book is to present a case example that illustrates how a person-centered therapist might work with a client, from case conceptualization to an actual counseling session.

Many if the core concepts of Person-Centered Counseling are presented, but this book is not intended to provide the reader with a thorough examination of the theory. Instead, it is meant to provide an example of the theory being applied to an actual client.

PERSONAL PHILOSOPHY

Human beings are complex and unique creatures. Each person is different in the way he or she experiences the world. It would be easy to list dozens of aspects that make each of us unique, but in order to gain an understanding of human nature, I believe it is most important to focus on what makes people alike. In addition, I believe each of us has an internal need to better ourselves, and we naturally possess the desire to do, and be, better. This is very similar to the view of Carl Rogers (1961), who asserted, "My experience has forced me to conclude that the individual has within himself the capacity and the tendency, latent if not evident, to move forward toward maturity" (p. 35). Rogers (as cited in Cain, 2010) called this constant need to improve oneself the *actualizing tendency*, or "the inherent tendency of the organism to develop all its capacities in ways which serve to maintain or enhance the organism" (p. 18).

More simply, people are driven to grow, become whole, and improve themselves.

I believe there exists within all of us an internal process that can motivate us to choose behaviors and actions that facilitate the actualizing tendency. This process is best described by Rogers's theory of the *organismic valuing process*. According to Hergenhahn and Olson (2003), in the organismic valuing process, when experiences are satisfying, we tend to approach and maintain them, which is in accordance with the actualizing tendency; however, "those experiences that are contrary to the actualizing tendency are unsatisfying and therefore are avoided or terminated" (p. 470). This allows a person to act in ways most beneficial to him by utilizing internal knowledge created by his organismic valuing system (Cain, 2010).

Beginning in early childhood, a person begins to develop a sense of self. Interactions with people close to a developing child allow the child to begin to see himself as an individual (Monte & Sollod, 2003). According to Hergenhahn and Olson (2003):

> At first, infants do not distinguish between events in their phenomenological field; the events blend together in a single configuration. Gradually, however, through experiences with verbal labels such as 'me' and 'I,' a portion of their phenomenological field becomes differentiated as the self. At this point, a person can reflect on himself or herself as a distinct object of which he or she is aware. (p. 471)

The actualizing tendency, which drives a person toward higher levels of maturity, facilitates the development of the sense of self (Hergenhahn & Olson, 2003). As a sense of self develops, a need for positive regard emerges (Monte & Sollod, 2003). I believe that all people have a need to feel valued, loved, appreciated, cared for, and respected.

Like Rogers, I, too, believe each individual experiences the world in ways unique to him or her. As Rogers (1980) revealed, the "only reality you can possibly know is the world as you perceive and experience it at that moment. And the only certainty is that those perceived realities are different. There are as many 'real worlds' as there are people!" (p. 102). Therefore, in order to understand the behaviors of an individual, an attempt must be made to understand reality from the individual's unique subjective view (Wade & Tavris, 2003).

Key Variables Affecting Psychological Health and Dysfunction

As a child develops a need for positive regard, he learns there are certain conditions in which positive regard is experienced. Conversely, he learns there are also conditions in which positive regard will not be experienced. When internalized through repeated experiences, these conditions determine a child's sense of worth and become part of his self-structure; once internalized, the conditions of worth "become a conscience, or superego, guiding the children's behavior even when the parents are not present" (Hergenhahn & Olson, 2003, p. 472). Because a person is likely to behave in ways in order to receive acceptance or praise from an important other, Cain (2010) warned this need for approval can become problematic if the person "disregards whether or not the behavior enhances his or her self, growth, or well-being" (p. 23). Such a person has developed conditions of worth yet abandoned his organismic valuing process. For example, a young boy might stop playing with dolls even though he may have initially found such play to be highly satisfying, because his parents disapprove of him playing with "girly" toys. Subsequently, the boy comes to dislike dolls because he has learned playing with them will not bring him positive regard, while playing with more "manly" toys will.

When these types of conditions of worth have developed, a person becomes incongruent. As explained by Hergenhahn and Olson (2003),

Incongruency exists when people no longer use their organismic valuing process as a means of determining if their experiences are in accordance with their actualizing tendency. If people do not use their own valuing process for evaluating their experiences, then they must be using someone's introjected values in doing so. (p. 473).

This means an incongruent person evaluates his experiences based on conditions of worth, which "represents a state of discord between the self-concept and experience" (Cain, 2010, p. 20).

Although he may be initially unaware of this discord, an incongruent person becomes susceptible to anxiety and distress. Feelings of insecurity and uncertainty can predominate, and the person can experience confusion and vulnerability regarding his sense of self (Cain, 2010).

PRACTICE OF THERAPY

When working with a client, my initial goal involves developing a solid therapeutic relationship. In order to build an alliance, it is important to create an environment in which the client can feel free to express himself without fear of judgment. Provided with such an environment, I believe a client has within him or her self the necessary tools and the desire for achieving personal growth. For this reason, I do not set rigid goals for a client. Nor do I follow a specific structured list of tasks. Instead, I believe a counselor must work to maintain an environment that fosters personal growth within the client. The key factors of a growth-fostering environment are empathy, genuineness, and non-judgmental acceptance of the client and his experiences (Fall, Miner, & Marquis, 2010, p. 182).

A client's progress toward desired outcomes will often become evident in two ways. First, it is important to check with the client periodically so he can provide a report to indicate his progress or regression. Because a client experiences his reality and the problems within it in ways unique to him, a self-reported progress report is, in my opinion, the best means of measuring progress. Second, in general, a client will show progress by beginning to operate in ways that serve his true self through facilitating personal growth. In other words, a client's actions will meet his own needs and will no longer be motivated by a need to meet certain expectations or adhere to the values of others.

Goals for Therapy

My general goals for therapy are best supported by the person-centered approach. Rogers' (1993) central hypothesis established that the individual carries "vast resources for self-understanding, for altering his or her self-concept, attitudes, and self-directed behavior — and that these resources can be tapped if only a definable climate of facilitative psychological attitudes can be provided" (p. 197). In other words, the client has an innate power to change and can access this inner power when his therapist creates an atmosphere conducive to a strong therapeutic relationship. Furthering support for the importance of the therapeutic relationship, Cain (2010) agreed: "The fundamental goal of person-centered therapists is the creation of an optimal therapeutic relationship for their clients" (p. 17). The therapeutic relationship is the most important factor in successful psychotherapy (Norcross, 2010).

According to Rogers (1980, 1993), there are three basic conditions that need to be present in order to provide a therapeutic climate that will facilitate growth. The first condition is the need to show genuineness with the client, to be real in a way that shows affinity, or what Rogers (1980) called *congruence*. When the therapist sits across from the client as himself, without putting up a façade or hiding behind a professional demeanor, the client is more likely to move toward change. Rogers (1980) described the second necessary element as *unconditional positive regard*, which involves accepting, caring for, and prizing—or valuing—the client, and he believed "when the therapist is experiencing a positive, acceptant attitude toward whatever the client *is* at that moment, therapeutic movement or change is more likely to occur" (p. 116). The third condition necessary to facilitate growth, as explained by Rogers (1980), is *empathic understanding*, where the therapist works to reflect accurately the client's experience, including what the client is feeling and the personal meanings the client attempts to communicate.

PSYCHOTHERAPY CASE

The basic philosophy of the person-centered approach involves providing an environment in which personal growth is facilitated (Rogers, 1993). Therefore, my ultimate goal as a counselor is to create a space in which the client feels accepted, accurately understood, and not judged. By providing an environment of congruence, unconditional positive regard, and empathic understanding, I believe the client has the opportunity to discover and express his true self, without feeling pressured by the introjected values or expectations of others. According to Truscott (2010), "in person-centered therapy, change occurs by shedding the self one is not and becoming one's true self" (p. 71).

My overall goals for the client presented in this paper were to create the conditions needed in order to foster growth and change. Rogers (1957) maintained there are six therapeutic conditions necessary for constructive therapeutic change to occur, and these must be present and consistent over time. These conditions are:

1. Two persons are in psychological contact.

2. The first, whom we shall term the client, is in a state of incongruence, being vulnerable or anxious.

3. The second person, whom we shall term the therapist, is congruent or integrated in the relationship.

4. The therapist experiences unconditional positive regard for the client.

5. The therapist experiences an empathic understanding of the client's internal frame of reference and endeavors to communicate this experience to the client.

6. The communication to the client of the therapist's empathic understanding and unconditional positive regard is to a minimal degree achieved. No other conditions are necessary. If these six

conditions exist, and continue over a period of time, this is sufficient. The process of constructive personality change will follow. (Rogers, 1957, p. 96)

These six elements expand upon the three so-called "core conditions" of empathy, unconditional positive regard, and congruence (Cain, 2010).

Efficacy

According to Cain (2010), research focused on the three necessary conditions of therapist empathy, unconditional positive regard, and congruence, and client outcome showed positive results. Rudolph, Langer, and Tausch (1980; as cited in Kirschenbaum & Jourdan, 2005) reported on a study involving 149 clients and 80 client-centered therapists that found "significant improvement in clients took place when therapists demonstrated [at least] two of the three core conditions" (p. 43). In a meta-analysis of 22 studies, Gurman (1977; as cited in Hergenhahn & Olson, 2003) found that clients who believed their therapists had provided genuineness, empathy, and unconditional positive regard were more likely to view the outcome of therapy as effective.

As reported by Cain (2010), research over approximately the past 60 years has revealed that person-centered therapy is an effective approach for the problems people most often seek therapy for; however, there are limitations in the scope of practice of person-centered therapy. For person-centered therapy to be effective, the client must have the capacity to be motivated to change (Cain, 2010). In addition, Cain (2010) noted, "persons with psychological disorders with a primary or strong biological component such as autism, severe and chronic schizophrenic disorders, panic disorder, pain disorders, severe mental retardation, and Tourette's disorder are probably not ideally suited to person-centered therapy" (p. 137). Further limitations include clients with disorders that are typically treated more successfully with behavioral interventions, such as obsessive–compulsive disorder and phobias (Cain, 2010).

Assessment

The client is a 21-year-old Caucasian female. At the time of her last session with this author, she was living with her romantic partner, a 21-year-old male. The client completed the requirements for her high-school diploma at the age of 21 and was attending classes at a community college at the time of last contact with this writer. The client is of low socioeconomic status and unemployed.

The client was adopted at the age of 16. She has one biological brother, age 15, and two adoptive sisters, both teenagers. She lived with her adoptive mother and father until moving in with her boyfriend several months before beginning therapy. The client is in regular contact with her biological mother after several years of no contact. The client's biological father is recently deceased.

Presenting problem

At the time of the initial assessment, the client reported feeling depressed all day, almost every day and stated the duration of the depressed mood had been approximately one year. She described feelings of hopelessness and guilt, and experienced irritability, anhedonia, trembling, frequent worry, and hypersensitivity. The client also reported nightmares, flashbacks, and emotional and physical arousal when reminded of trauma, as well as avoidance of reminders of trauma for approximately three weeks. The trauma consisted of the client finding her aunts body after an accidental death. In addition, she endorsed a decreased interest in important activities, feeling detached from others, affective numbing, foreshortened sense of future, pronounced fatigue, insomnia and episodic early awakening, decreased appetite, weight loss, and impairments in short-term memory and concentration.

The client reported she was seeking help due to difficulties in coping with the recent deaths of two relatives, and noted her adoptive mother had encouraged her to seek help. She explained she would be starting college approximately one month after the initial assessment and believed therapy would help her successfully complete her college education. Working to overcome depression was her stated goal for therapy.

The client's initial assessment was administered by an intake clinician. Because clients at this agency are routinely asked if they have a gender preference for their counselor, and the client reported no gender preference, the intake clinician referred her to this writer as the next available counselor.

Behavioral observations

The client's appearance, behavior, mood, thought process, and affect were within normal limits. She appeared to be in good health and reported no significant health problems. Physical coordination and cognitive functioning appeared to be within normal limits as well. The client often looked down while speaking and generally avoided eye contact. The client's speech was soft. This client did not report any suicidal or homicidal ideations.

History

The client reported growing up in a very small town. Both her mother and father were alcoholics, and they divorced when she was very young. In addition, she was physically and emotionally abused by her father and neglected by her mother. Her mother and younger brother continue to abuse alcohol. The client disclosed frequent involvement with the juvenile justice system beginning at the age of 13, and several arrests for assaults and drug possession. She reported a history of abusing methamphetamine, completion of chemical dependency treatment, and last use of methamphetamine at the age of 16.

Due to the abuse of drugs and her involvement with law enforcement, the client was sent to live with a family friend more than 250 miles from her home. This family friend then adopted the client. The client had little contact with her biological family for the next two years, but following her 18th birthday, she resumed regular contact with her biological mother and brother. Because they have not forgiven her for her previous actions, the client does not speak with most of her extended family.

The client disclosed she was pushed out of a moving vehicle by her father when she was 14 years old. However, according to the client, neither her family nor the medical staff believed her when she accused her father of having pushed her out of the car. Her injuries were minor, but she was hospitalized because the medical staff thought she was at risk of hurting herself. Before being adopted, the client stabbed her biological mother's abusive boyfriend with a knife. She claimed self-defense and was not charged with a crime; however, she stated she does not believe the stabbing was an act of self-defense because she was protecting her mother, not herself.

The client reported a history of self-harm. The client disclosed she cut herself with a pocketknife on three occasions when she was 14-years-old. The cuts were not deep enough to require medical attention. The client stated that she had not cut herself since she was 14-years-old and would not engage in self-harm in the future.

Approximately one year before beginning therapy, the client reported she fell from a considerable height while rock climbing and suffered a traumatic brain injury. She was in a coma for several days and remained hospitalized for approximately one month.

More recently, the client discovered the body of her adoptive aunt after an apparent accidental prescription medication overdose. Because the medication had been prescribed to the client, she believed her adoptive mother blamed her for the death. In addition, the client's biological father was in a motorcycle accident in 2009 that left him in a vegetative state until he died, approximately two weeks after the client began therapy. The client reported she had not spoken with her father since the accident, as her father's wife would not allow it.

Diagnosis

It should be noted that making a formal diagnosis using the *Diagnostic and Statistical Manual of Mental Disorders* (5th ed.; *DSM–5*; American Psychiatric Association [APA], 2013) is not a goal of a person-centered therapist as it is not believed to be beneficial to treatment (Corey, 2005). Diagnosing a client can lead to the therapist focusing on those aspects of a client that confirm the diagnosis while ignoring other aspects (Yalom, 2009). This inhibits the ability of a therapist to understand the client from the client's true point of view.

Although I do not believe in making formal diagnoses, the diagnosis on the following page would likely be appropriate for insurance billing purposes.

Possible Diagnosis

296.33	Major Depressive Disorder, Recurrent, Severe
308.3	Acute Stress Disorder (R/O 309.81, Posttraumatic Stress Disorder, Acute)
304.40	Amphetamine Dependence, Sustained Full Remission

(APA, 2013)

Case Formulation

After several sessions working the client, I began to notice a major theme: The client's fear of failure. The client frequently spoke about failures in her past, such as dropping out of school, her involvement with the juvenile justice system as a result of poor decision-making, her drug use as a teenager, and the possibility, even likelihood, of failing in the future. Over time, I observed central to this theme of failure was her fear and anxiety over what her family might think of her should she fail again in the future.

Because several members of her family, especially her adoptive and biological mothers, frequently made her feel guilty about her past failures and expressed doubts that she would be able to achieve her current and future goals, such as finishing college, the client frequently stated she could not bear the thought of failing again in front of her family. I began to understand how what the client's family was telling her about herself—that she had been and would continue to be a failure—did not match who the client believed her true self to be. This incongruence placed the client in a state of confusion, anxiety, and depression. Although she had failures in her past, the client was taking steps to meet her current goals. By reminding her of past failures and doubting her ability to achieving her more recent goals, her family has caused the client to question, internally, whether or not being a failure is consistent with her true self, or if it is simply a part of her past.

I believe the client has allowed her family to determine her conditions of worth. The client often described her adoptive mother as controlling, noting her adoptive mother makes many decisions for her and financially supports her. For example, the client reported she would like to be more financially independent and not accept help from her adoptive mother, yet when she wanted to seek employment, her adoptive mother would not let her. She noted she has felt obligated to help her adoptive mother whenever she is asked, and she admitted she "would feel bad" if she sought more financial independence. In order to be accepted, the client has attempted to be the version of a daughter that her adoptive mother wants; however, she has continued denying her own needs in order to gain the approval of her adoptive mother. Clearly, the client is not doing what she believes would be most beneficial for her own sense of self.

Another example of the client allowing another person to determine her conditions of worth can be found in her relationship with her biological mother. The client reported her mother failed to give her adequate attention when she was a child, often leaving her at home alone and neglected. She also believed the roles of mother and daughter were reversed. Based on the client's description of her relationship with her mother, both as a child and at the time of therapy, it is my opinion that her mother demands that the client be available to her emotionally and financially, but she does not make herself available to the client. Even though the client is unemployed and cannot always meet her own financial needs, she reported feeling obligated to help her mother financially. I believe the client is behaving according to the conditions for acceptance that have been set by her mother.

During our first session, the client remained skeptical of therapy and expressed her dislike of talking about her problems. She recalled seeing a therapist as a teenager, which she described as a negative experience, and reported some anxiety surrounding the possibility that attending therapy a second time might result in another negative experience. Despite her initial hesitation, she stated she was eager to overcome her symptoms and would keep an open mind about the process. I encouraged her to inform me if, at any time, she felt the therapy process was not serving her needs or if she had any other concerns.

Recommendations

The person-centered approach does not stress the application of specific or structured interventions. Instead, as Truscott (2010) proposed, "in person-centered therapy, change occurs by shedding the self one is not and becoming one's true self" (p. 71). However, there are certain areas of concern that might be appropriate to focus on during therapy with this client in order to allow the client to discover her true self.

For example, I believe it would be helpful to explore her relationships with her family and the conditions of worth operating within those relationships. Specifically, it would likely be beneficial for the client to dissect her relationships with her mothers. This might allow the client to determine for herself if building healthier relationships with her mother and adoptive mother, relationships in which the client would have greater independence, would contribute to her personal growth.

Another issue worth exploring with this client is the theme of failure, which reappears with some frequency. This could allow the client to shed the label of failure from her perceived self. It would be helpful to work with the client on reframing her perceived failures as opportunities for growth and learning.

Progress Report

Through using a person-centered approach to therapy with the client, I believe I was able to create an environment in which she began to feel free to communicate openly. In short, the plan for therapy was to build a strong therapeutic relationship by providing a setting where the client would not feel judged, would feel accepted, and would feel as though she was positively regarded by her therapist. By creating a growth-fostering environment, I hoped to open up new possibilities for her where she would begin to make decisions based on her own needs, rather than on the approval of others. More precisely, she would begin to utilize her own organismic valuing process.

Early in therapy, during the first two sessions, the client remained reluctant to share her emotions or to speak about herself and her problems. However, her initial apprehension began to fade as the therapeutic relationship strengthened, and after several sessions, the client began to speak more openly and to share her emotions. In addition, early in therapy the client would often change the topic when something would trigger an emotional response. Over time, the frequency of the client changing the topic when it became uncomfortable for her was reduced as she began to feel accepted and not judged.

As therapy progressed, the client began to make changes that served to improve herself, rather than trying to meet the expectations of others. One example of this: She chose to change her educational goals, despite the disapproval of her adoptive mother who wanted her to study for a career in healthcare. Instead, she has decided to pursue a career in law enforcement because she finds that field to be personally fulfilling. Following this decision, the client reported a reduction of feelings of hopelessness, and she began to speak about her future and the exciting possibilities that lie ahead. In my opinion, changing her college and career goals to better suit her desires empowered the client to think about taking charge of her future.

The client also made progress regarding her feelings of guilt by beginning to let go of the self-blame she felt regarding the accidental death of her adoptive aunt. Based on my observations, she began to realize that being capable of causing the death of her aunt was not consistent with the person she truly believed herself to be.

As previously mentioned, I asked the client during our first session to inform me if it any time something was not working in therapy. Initially, the client had agreed to attend weekly sessions. However, after the sixth or seventh session, she stated she would feel more comfortable meeting less often. She revealed that talking about her personal problems was emotionally draining for her because it was something she was not used to doing, and doing so every week was causing her distress. She requested that future appointments be scheduled on a bi-weekly basis. In order to meet the needs of the client, all future sessions were scheduled for every other week.

Due to funding issues at the agency in which our therapy took place, continued work with the client was not an option. For this reason, I referred the client to resources available in her community, including free crisis intervention and low cost counseling services. If funding had not been an issue, I believe the client would have benefited from continued therapy, and had it been possible, I would have preferred to see the client for several more sessions Although she did make significant progress, as evidenced by symptom rating scales the client completed during each session, a longer course of therapy would have likely produced greater progress. The area deserving ongoing focus would have likely been the client's fear of failure. When therapy ended, the client self-reported she still struggled with the fear of failure, although it had been reduced.

Counseling Session Transcript

T = Therapist

C = Client

T1   **So, tell me about your, it's been two weeks, right?**

C1   Yeah. [Laughs]

T2   So it sounds like there's been a lot going on.

C2   Mmhmm (yes). I started school. That's been okay except I didn't go this morning. So, but yeah, me and [boyfriend] are splitting up, so I think I might have to move. And he's been abusive to [client's dog], so I guess it's

---

good that we're splitting up.

T3 You guess it's good?

C3 (nods) He hit [dog] yesterday.

T4 And just so I get it right, [name of dog] is

your dog, right?

C4 (nods)

T5 Okay.

C5 Yeah, but she's like everything to me and

I would choose her over anybody.

T6 (Nods)

C6 I'm thinking about moving to [City]. But,

I know that [adoptive Mother] doesn't

want me to but my Mom does.

T7 Your mom wants you to move back?

C7 (Nods) Yeah. I don't know. If I lived in [City], I'd be able to get a job. So, it wouldn't be as horrible as living in [City]. And, I'd still be really close to her. Or I can move in with my Dad's wife. But. Yeah, I don't know what to do.

T8 Sounds like you've got a few options there.

C8 Yeah, but they're all far away.

T9 (Nod)

C9 (Silence) Is that outside (sound of rain)?

T10 (Nods yes)

C10 It wasn't raining when I came in.

T11 I don't think so, yeah. (Long silence). So

what do you think you'll end up doing,

or what are you leaning toward?

C11 I have no idea what I'm going to do. I

haven't decided yet. If I leave, I'm going

to have to quit school and go to school

somewhere else.

T12 Mmhmm (yes). And I know you were

looking forward to school for a long

time, right?

C12 I was very happy to go yesterday. Very

happy. But, every time I start something,

something like this seems to go on.

Nothing ever goes my way. Everything is

challenge. It makes me want to give up

on things.

T13 But you haven't (given up), right?

C13 Not yet, but I'm really close. I started search training, but I don't know if I'm going to keep doing that now because, I don't know. One, I don't want to see him [boyfriend] there, which hopefully he will stop going. And two, if I leave I can't do it and then I'll lose that chance to get that opportunity as Homeland Security. And, I don't want to move back to [adoptive Mother's house]. [Dog] doesn't like it there and it's too chaotic and disgusting to live there.

T14 You've got a lot on your plate right now.

C14 Again? Do I ever come here with good news? (Laughs).

T15 (Laughs). Yeah, you've come with some good news.

C15 Really?

T16 Mmhmm (yes).

C16 Why can't I remember anything good?

T17 You had good news last week. Or, two weeks ago when you were here, I should say.

C17 What was that?

T18 You had school, uhm, you were excited about the possibility of looking into the

National Guard.

C18 (Starts crying).

T19 What are you thinking about?

C19 Uhm, how everything happened.

T20 What's everything?

C20 Just how I ended up here.

T21 Here like this building, or here in your situation that you're in.

C21 Situation. Everybody's pulling me in different directions. Everybody except my Mom lays guilt trips on me. All I want to do is move back, but I can't because, I don't know. Everybody would be pissed off at me.

T22   Sounds like you're just stuck.

C22   Yeah, I am. And, if it wasn't for [my

dog], I'd probably like join the Military

and leave. But, I can't leave her with just

anybody and I know how she reacts

when I'm not there. She's the only one

that hasn't screwed me over. That's

saying a lot.

T23   You said that you want to move back to

[City], but everyone will be mad at you.

What do you think would happen if you

went?

C23   I think that they wouldn't stop calling

me and I think that maybe I'm afraid of

failing without them. And I'm afraid that I might meet someone over there that I was trying to forget and then I'll make myself stuck again. And, [City] is not the place to go to get a career. So, I'm afraid if I might that decision it's going to be the worst one I've ever made.

T24 You sound really scared.

C24 I've been this scared a couple times and it never turned out good. I almost didn't come today, again.

T25 Is it difficult for you to talk about these things?

C25 Yeah. I don't like crying, it makes me

kind of mad. And every time I try

holding it back, it just hurts. I don't really

like people helping me with my

problems, I guess.

T26 I just want to go back for a second, you

said that you were afraid to fail without

the people around you, I guess to

support you, right?

C26 Mmhmm (yes), because I'm in school

and I can't lose my grant, or else I can't

go to school.

T27 So, you don't like people helping you,

but you…

C27 Only one person, I guess, and I still don't

like her helping me. But, I don't have any other choice and she actually brought it upon herself because she actually got angry when I wanted a job and it turned into a huge fight and I guess I just gave up and now I'm just used to it. I don't want her help, I want to be able to do everything myself. But, I feel bad if I tell her I don't want help. But, with my Mom, I know she can't help so I'll be doing everything on my own. And, I actually help my Mom. I make money, I bought her a new laptop for her business and I'd rather support her than have someone help me. And, I'm afraid to be a

failure in front of her since I've already

done that. I don't want it to happen

again.

T28 I'm hearing a lot about failure.

C28 Yeah. I guess maybe I fail because I think

about it too much, but it's a little hard

because I've never succeeded until now.

T29 So you feel like you don't spend enough

time thinking about what if things work

out the right way, the way I want it...

C29 I never do. I can't remember the last time

I actually said that, or thought that. It

took me until I was 20, 21 to finish high

school. That was a failure, but then I finished high school even though I thought it was still a failure because I could have been in my third year of college or something and I would be okay right now. I wouldn't be needing someone's help. I think about if I would have stayed with my Dad, even though he was a jerk, I probably would be more successful because as soon as I lived with my Mom I dropped out. [I] moved in with my boyfriend. Things have never gone okay. It's kind of hard to train my brain to tell me that it's going to be okay.

T30 Well, I've seen you with that attitude before when you were talking about things that you could do for your...

C30 Really?

T31 ...Career. Yeah.

C31 Yeah, but...

T32 You were pretty hopeful.

C32 How long did that last?

T33 I don't know.

C33 A very short amount of time. Well, since yesterday anyway. I mean yesterday was awesome until I got home and then everything just blew up. I guess it's good that we didn't get married. So, people

PERSON-CENTERED COUNSELING

say that it's not good to live with

someone before you get married, but I

think it was the best choice. So I guess

that's positive. And this is the hardest

relationship though because he was

actually nice except for that fact that he

hit my dog last night. But, all my other

boyfriends were either too controlling or

too abusive and I've only had four, so.

Yeah, I don't know.

T34 So is it more difficult for you to think

about ending this relationship because he

was not abusive like your past

boyfriends?

C34 I really liked him except for his urge not to do laundry, or the dishes, or come up with rent which I had to do and it was not very easy because I don't have a job. But, he was the best one I had because I haven't really been with someone who was there for me and he was a little bit, but I think I could do better.

T35 What would that look like, doing better?

C35 Someone who is successful. Someone who doesn't get mad at the smallest things and someone who is responsible and actually helps clean up the house and has rent on time and someone who respects me for who I am. I don't, I think he's scared of my past, which I am too, but I don't know, maybe I should lie to the next guy.

T36 Lie, why? So they don't know…

C36 Who I was, What I put myself through, how I made my life miserable, like for years. I can't remember not regretting anything in my life. Like I regret everything.

T37 That's a lot of, that's a big burden to have.

C37 Yeah, I can't even see any of the good images. All I see is everything that's bad.

Thanks for shopping with us.
Kindest Regards, Customer Care

RETURNING GOODS

Please re-pack, in the original packaging if possible, and send back to us at the address below. **Caution!** Don't cover up the barcode (on original packaging) as it helps us to process your return.

We will email you when we have processed your return.

✂ -

PLEASE complete and include this section with your goods.

Your Name _____

Your Order Number _____

Reason for Return _____

Would you prefer: Refund ⊟ or Replacement ☐

(Please note, if we are unable to replace the item it will be refunded.)

Return to:

✂ -

> **RETURNS**
> 801 Penhorn Avenue, Unit 5
> Secaucus
> NJ
> 07094

T38 And you wish you could see the good?

C38 Might make me a little happier. A little

more hopeful.

T39 So what would have to change to allow

you to see the good?

C39 I have no idea. I don't even know where

to start. I had a test today about memory

with one of the state people that's

tracking my head injury and I failed

because I didn't remember anything.

Even in school, I'm afraid I'm not going

to remember anything they teach me.

T40 What if you do?

C40 Remember?

T41 (nods yes)

C41 I hope it's good. I hope there's something good about my childhood or being with my Mother. And, usually the only thing I can remember are the things I dream about. Like I can't remember any one week, I can only remember parts of like a year. It's very frustrating. It makes my life really miserable.

T42 I want to go back to your Mom for second. I get the sense that you really want to move back there.

C42 I do.

T43 But, but you're being held back.

C43 Yep, by many things. If I do move back I couldn't stay with her because of the dogs, but I have other family up there. My Grandma and my Uncles. But, there's a lot of memories up there and none of them are good.

T44 It sounds like you miss your family, but there's a lot of things that happened there that you don't want to have to remember.

C44 It's really hard to walk down the streets. It's a very small town and like every street something horrible happened, either a murder or something that I remember and no matter how hard I try I can't remember anything good that's happened there, or with my Dad. But, [City is] like the one place I want to be.

T45 So it's like you really want to go but you don't at the same time.

C45 (Nods) I think that if I go two things could happen. I could end up really happy, or I could end up getting arrested again or freaking out. Or, start drinking heavily again because that's what my family does. My mom's cut back, but when I went back there my fifteen-year-old brother made me a "splodie," which is like six different kinds of alcohol.

T46 So you're afraid of what you might do?

C46 I don't want to hurt my family. Again, anyway. I've already punched my Mom's boyfriend, or husband. He still likes me, but just the smallest thing can make me hurt someone.

T47 You said the smallest thing. What was the small thing that made that happen?

C47 Uhm, they were drinking and, this doesn't happen all the time but, he got a little verbally abusive towards her and ever since I moved in with her I've been too protective I guess. It's not the first husband I've beat. But, I just got angry and she just started crying when he came back out. I just hit him and then her previous boyfriend I stabbed because he was being abusive toward her. And luckily I got self-defense.

T48 Was it self-defense?

C48 No, no it wasn't. He fought back, but it was just, I mean it can't be self-defense if he was just saying words.

T49 Well words can hurt pretty bad.

C49 Yeah, but you can't stab someone. There was blood all over, but my Mom stood by me. But, he made it, so it's not like I killed somebody. And then I've cut in front of my little brother. He forgives me, but I guess I haven't yet.

T50 You haven't forgiven yourself?

C50 Not even close (long pause). I think that's what's stopping me because I don't want to hurt them again. But, they want me to (forgive myself). They're the only part of my family that's actually forgiven me for what I've done. Other than my cousins on my Dad's side, but those are the only ones on my Dad's side that's forgiven me. And I did worse things when I was with my Mom than I did when I was with my Dad because my Dad was the

one who was abusive. And everyone

blames me for moving away. And his

wife was abusive. I went to a mental

health facility for jumping out of a

moving vehicle, but I was pushed. But,

no one believed a fourteen-year-old. It's

almost time.

T51 You want it to be over?

C51 (Nods yes).

T52 It's hard talking about these things for

you.

C52 (Long pause, crying) Yes it is.

T53 Sounds like you went through a lot when

you were younger.

C53 Yeah, well.

T54 A lot of terrible things.

C54 I'm trying to make everything better, but

it's not working.

T55 But you're trying, right?

C55 Yeah. I am doing that.

T56 It takes a lot to try, a lot of guts. It would

be a lot easier just to give up, right?

C56 Yeah, which I'm trying really hard not to

do. Like a really hard part is winning, I

think.

T57 It's hard to see yourself winning?

C57 Yeah (long pause).

T58   We talked about a lot today.

C58   I'm surprised, actually.

T59   Why?

C59   Because I didn't even want to come in the first place. And, I absolutely despise crying; I find it to be weak.

T60   And you don't like feeling weak. You want to feel strong all the time.

C60   Yeah. I never cried once when I got arrested or for stabbing, or for punching [Mom's Husband].

T61   Well then, I would think that allowing yourself to cry is probably a pretty strong thing, right?

C61 No.

T62 But it's not easy for you.

C62 No, it's not. So are you saying it was easy for me to stab someone (laughs)?

T63 No.

C63 Or easy for me to get arrested? Which it was easy, but I think the only reason I got arrested was because it was safe and I knew, like, the staff members, they were like my family and the police officers were like my family and they allowed me to go their house even after I was arrested. And they all got pissed at me, which was good. And they all followed me, even when I didn't know it, so they could arrest my boyfriend because I wouldn't tell them. But, now I don't have them because I left and freaked out because I thought someone was after me and I was at their house. And [ex-boyfriend], I don't think, ever forgave me. But, maybe one of these days you'll convince me that crying is a sign of strength, but not today.

T64 Well, at least you're open to it.

C64 Yes, I am open to it. I'm not saying it will work right away, but maybe eventually. But, I'm not saying that because I think it's a sign of strength when I cry all the

time because that still won't happen. But,

I'll try. It's time, exactly. And three text

messages that are probably not good.

T65 Well, I'll let you get out of here.

C65 Okay. Next week same time?

T66 Yeah.

C66 Okay.

Analysis of Therapy Process

The beginning of the presented session was somewhat awkward for both the client and this writer. I believe the awkwardness and anxiety evident was due to the change in the counseling environment brought on by the video camera that recorded the session. I sensed the anxiety in the room and debated about whether or not I should acknowledge it. When the client looked at the camera and nervously smiled before any conversation had started, my automatic reaction was to begin the session in order to quell my own anxiety. In retrospect, I should have acknowledged the anxiety. By not acknowledging it, I was being disingenuous. If I had been genuine, by accepting and communicating the feelings present for both myself and the client, the session would have most likely had a smoother beginning.

At T1 (refer to transcript), I started the session by vaguely asking the client how the previous two weeks had gone for her. I felt it was important to ask because it had been two weeks since the last session, instead of the usual one week. However, I did not phrase the question clearly. Instead of saying, "How have the last two weeks been?" it came out as "Tell me about your, it's been two weeks, right?" The client answered my question about the passage of time, rather than what I actually meant to ask, which was to find out if having two weeks between sessions had been helpful for her. I interpreted the client's laugh at C1 as her indication that several events had transpired since the previous session. My response at T2, "So it sounds like ..." was meant to let the client know I understood the meaning of her laughter.

During the beginning of the session, I attempted to use reflective responses in order for the client to feel I was truly listening to her. At T3, I reflected how the client felt, that ending her relationship with her boyfriend was a positive thing. At C3, the client reported her boyfriend had been abusive toward her dog.

At first, I was unsure if she was referring to her dog, so at T4, I asked a clarifying question. At T7, I reflected to the client how her mother wanted her to move back to her hometown. In using reflective responses, I was attempting to withhold any judgment while encouraging the client to elaborate.

At C29, the client said, "I never do…." Here she was relaying how things never seem to work out for her, and how it is difficult for her to be hopeful that things will work out the way she wants them to. At T30, I felt the need to rescue the client by telling her I had seen her expressing a hopeful attitude in previous sessions. I wanted to challenge her statement and tell her that she was wrong—that she is hopeful at times and things do sometimes work out in a positive manner. I think my comments at T30 and T31 caused the client to become defensive at C30 and C31. At T32, I continued to challenge her: "You were pretty hopeful." At C32, the client continued to be defensive by replying, "How long did that last?" I realized the interaction was becoming counterproductive, so I retreated at T33. At C33 and T34 the topic moved in a different direction.

Although my intentions were positive, by challenging the client I believe I had invalidated her feelings. I was, in effect, setting conditions for acceptance by essentially implying how I thought she should feel, rather than understanding how she truly felt. My comments also possibly implied judgment. Perhaps a more effective response would have been to acknowledge her feelings in an empathic, understanding manner. Reflecting back to the client a statement such as, "You feel like no matter how hard you try you will fail and it won't work out the way that you would like it to," would have been more productive. Responding in such a way might have allowed the client to feel understood.

At C49, the client stated, "Yeah, but you can't…." Here, she was speaking about stabbing her biological mother's boyfriend and cutting herself (years earlier) in front of her younger brother. She mentioned her brother had forgiven her, but she had not forgiven herself. I suspected she was referring to more than cutting in front of her brother when she mentioned forgiveness. In my response at T50, "You haven't forgiven yourself," I was attempting to respond without judgment. I felt it was important to acknowledge that I understood the importance of the client's statement. This was the first time in therapy the client had indicated she could not forgive herself for some actions in her past. I believe her long pause at C50 was an indication that she was beginning to see the importance of forgiving herself. It was clear my response at T50 had stirred an emotional response, as the client began to tear up. She went on to state, at C50, that some members of her family had forgiven her, but few family members on her Father's side had. She pointed out her Mother's side of the family was able to forgive her for actions of greater severity, yet her Father's side would not forgive her for actions of lesser severity. I think these comments represent the client's need for approval.

At the end of C50, the client looked at her phone and said, "It's almost time." It was clear to me that the client felt vulnerable after speaking about painful events in her past and her need for forgiveness. In my statement at T51, "You want it to be over," I was attempting to be caring and accepting of the client, while accurately understanding and communicating what she was feeling. She agreed by nodding. In order to offer the client a sense of safety in speaking about emotionally difficult topics, I continued to use empathic understanding at T52: "It's hard talking about...." At C52, the client paused, began to cry, and said "Yes it is." I interpreted the long pause and tears as the client thinking about her past, and I wanted to convey to the client that she was understood, so at T53, I empathized, "Sounds like you went through a lot when you were younger." At C53, the client replied, "Yeah, well," and shrugged her shoulders. I took this to mean the client was minimizing her feelings about her past. At T54, when I noted, "A lot of terrible...," I continued to send the message that I understood her feelings in order to promote a feeling of safety.

In the session presented, one of the main issues addressed by the client was her fear of failure. She spoke about feeling she had never succeeded at anything. She regarded finishing high school late as a failure and the relationship with her boyfriend as a failure. In general, she saw failure as a theme in her life because to her, nothing ever seemed to work out positively. I believe through empathic understanding I was able to help the client gain some important personal insight. At C28, she admitted, "Yeah. I guess maybe I fail because I think about it too much."

Another main theme of the session was the client's ambivalence about moving back to her hometown. She had many negative experiences growing up there and was afraid of moving back, yet she missed her family, and a big part of her wanted to move back. As noted earlier, the client found it difficult to speak about the negative events in her past, and she sometimes avoided doing so. She expressed guilt about her past and fears of repeating past mistakes if she returned to her hometown. I found it important to interact with the client in a nonjudgmental and empathic manner in order for her to feel safe to speak about her past and her fears for the future.

Self-Evaluation

In my opinion, self-evaluating your work with a client is just as important as receiving feedback from a supervisor. I offer the following self-evaluation of my work to be used as a guideline for critiquing your own sessions with clients:

The supervision I received for the client presented was mainly focused on case management. My supervisor did, however, provide guidance on diversity issues, and I also sought supervision for countertransference issues. I do not recall encountering any ethical issues in my work with the client, as the relationship between the client and I was appropriately therapeutic and client confidentiality was respected.

At the beginning of the session I failed to acknowledge the anxiety in the room. Accepting and discussing the anxiety would have likely created a smoother start to the session. It might have eased the client's anxiety as well, possibly leading to a more productive session. My own anxiety prevented me from pointing it out. I felt somewhat embarrassed that I was experiencing anxiety in front of the client. I think I wanted her to see me as someone confident, someone who could help, and being anxious at the time contradicted the image I was trying to portray. I believe it is important for a therapist to be congruent and open to the feelings present in the therapy room. At the beginning, I failed to be genuine; however, I recovered from the initial incongruence and was able to provide a safe and productive environment.

As a person-centered therapist, I believe in a person's natural tendency toward growth. As such, I also believe it is important to allow the client to decide what topics will be addressed in session, as she knows best what is important to discuss. In this session, I feel like I allowed her to choose the issues to be addressed, except for those few moments when I lost focus and allowed my mind wander. At such times (T42, for example), I referred back to earlier discussion points to regain focus. I think I referred back to earlier comments because I did not want the client to know my mind had wandered and I had not been listening for a moment. Again, this is an issue of being incongruent. In retrospect, admitting I had missed something the client said might have been a better choice. Although I was congruent for the majority of the session, I am aware that had I been more consistently, and more continuously, congruent throughout the session, the clients experience could have possibly been a more productive one.

My main goal with this client was to develop a strong therapeutic relationship, as I believe the therapeutic relationship is the most important factor in therapy. Ultimately, I believe we developed a strong rapport. Although in earlier sessions the client was reluctant to open up and expose her vulnerabilities through revealing her emotions, by presenting myself as nonjudgmental, utilizing empathic listening, and showing positive regard, she became more comfortable in therapy. Over time, she began to share her emotions and spoke more openly about her troubled past and her current struggles. In the session presented, this is evidenced by the client speaking openly about some of her problems and allowing herself to cry, even though it was not easy for her to do so. I believe she had begun to trust me as her therapist.

I did not notice any issues of transference or countertransference in the session presented; however, such issues were evident in earlier sessions. In one session, the client became agitated when speaking about the death of her father. I had said something that reminded her of a family member who had blamed her for some of her father's problems. Also, in the first two sessions, I found myself feeling the urge to comfort and rescue the client when she spoke about the negative experiences in her past. I discussed this with my supervisor and came to realize that some of the client's experiences were similar to experiences I had as a child, and I was projecting my own personal feelings. Being aware of my own countertransference issues allowed me to recognize when it was occurring before the therapeutic relationship was damaged.

I think diversity issues possibly threatened the development of the therapeutic relationship very early in therapy. For example, the client is of low socioeconomic status, and during the first session she made a comment implying that someone in my position would not be able to understand her and the issues she had with her family. In the second session, in response to supervision I had received, I simply told the client I truly wanted to understand her, and I would do my best. I asked if that would be okay with her, and she said, "Yes." This seemed to put her at ease and the therapeutic relationship began to develop. Perhaps I am speculating, but the way I was dressed, in professional attire, may have caused her to think that someone of a higher socioeconomic status (the way that she perceived me) would not understand the problems unique to people of lower socioeconomic status, such as herself.

Overall, I was able to develop a strong therapeutic relationship, and I believe this session demonstrates how to conduct a productive psychotherapy session by providing an environment in which personal growth can flourish.

Critical Thinking Exercises

Counseling Responses

The session presented is not a perfect example of person-centered counseling, as, in my opinion, no such thing exists. Several of my responses to the client in the session were not representative of person-centered theory. Can you spot them? Refer to the transcript, find any responses that could be changed to better reflect a person-centered approach and draft your own responses in the space provided below (example: T34 might be considered a cognitive behavioral response).

_____

_____

_____

_____

_____

_____

_____

_____

Diagnosis

I previously mentioned my aversion to formal diagnoses. However, making a diagnosis is required in most agency settings so getting practice in this area can be beneficial. Formulate your own diagnosis for the client presented. How does it differ from the one provided in this book?

_____

_____

_____

_____

_____

_____

_____

_____

_____

_____

_____

_____

_____

References

American Psychiatric Association. (2013). Diagnostic and statistical manual of mental disorders (5th ed.). Washington, DC: Author.

Cain, D. J. (2010). Person-centered psychotherapies. Washington, DC: American Psychological Association.

Corey, G. (2005). Case approach to counseling and psychotherapy. Belmont, CA: Brooks/Cole.

Fall, K. A., Miner, H. J., & Marquis, A. (2010). Theoretical models of counseling and psychotherapy (2nd ed.). New York, NY: Routledge

Hergenhahn, B. R., & Olson, M. H. (2003). An introduction to theories of personality (6th ed.). Upper Saddle River, NJ: Prentice Hall.

References

Kirschenbaum, H., & Jourdan, A. (2005). The current status of Carl Rogers and the person-centered approach. Psychotherapy: Theory, Research, Practice, Training, 42, 37–51. doi:10.1037/0033-3204.42.1.37

Monte, C. F., & Sollod, R. N. (2003). Beneath the mask: An introduction to theories of personality (7th ed.). Hoboken, NJ: John Wiley & Sons.

Norcross, J. C (2010). The therapeutic relationship. In B.Duncan, S. Miller, B. Wampold, & M. Hubble (Eds.), The heart and soul of change: Delivering what works in therapy (113-142). Washington DC: American Psychological Association.

References

Rogers, C. R. (1957). The necessary and
	sufficient conditions of therapeutic
	personality change. Journal of
	Consulting Psychology, 21, 95–103.

Rogers, C. R. (1959). A theory of therapy,
	personality, and interpersonal
	relationships as developed in the client-
	centered framework. In S. Koch (Ed.),
	Psychology: A study of science, Vol. 3:
	Formulations of the person and the
	social context (pp. 184–256). New York,
	NY: McGraw-Hill.

Rogers, C. R. (1961). On becoming a person: A
	therapist's view of psychotherapy.
	Boston, MA: Houghton Mifflin.

Rogers, C. R. (1980). A way of being. Boston,
	MA: Houghton Mifflin.

References

Rogers, C. R. (1993). Client-centered therapy. In I. L. Kutash & A. Wolf (Eds.), Psychotherapist's casebook: Theory and technique in the practice of modern therapies (pp. 197–208). Northvale, NJ: Jason Aronson.

Truscott, D. (2010). Becoming an effective psychotherapist: Adopting a theory of psychotherapy that's right for you and your client. Washington, DC: American Psychological Association.

Wade, C., & Tavris, C. (2003). Psychology (7th ed.). Upper Saddle River, NJ: Prentice Hall.

Yalom, I., D. (2009). The gift of therapy: An open letter to a new generation of therapists and their patients. New York, NY: HarperCollins.